D0601887

ART CENTER COLLEGE OF DESIGN
3 3220 00095 1983

RAPHAEL SOYER

RAPHAEL SOYER

By LLOYD GOODRICH

PUBLISHED FOR THE
WHITNEY MUSEUM OF AMERICAN ART
BY FREDERICK A. PRAEGER, PUBLISHERS
NEW YORK · WASHINGTON · LONDON

Cover: OFFICE GIRLS. 1936. 26 x 24.
Collection of the Whitney Museum of American Art. Il. p. 42.

Frontispiece: SELF PORTRAIT. 1965. 16 x 20.
Collection of Joan and Lester Avnet.

Title Page: SELF PORTRAIT. c. 1927. 11 x 8¼.
The Phillips Collection.

Published in the United States of America in 1967
by FREDERICK A. PRAEGER, Inc., Publishers
111 Fourth Avenue, New York, N. Y. 10003
77-79 Charlotte Street, London W. 1, England
Library of Congress Catalog Card Number: 67-28775

Designed by Susan Draper Tundisi

Printed in the United States of America
by Publishers Printing-Admiral Press, New York

RAPHAEL SOYER

"My art is representational by choice," Raphael Soyer has written. "In my opinion, if the art of painting is to survive, it must describe and express people, their lives and times. It must communicate. . . . I consider myself a modern artist, or rather an artist of today, . . . because I am influenced by the thoughts, the life and the aesthetics of our time. I am also an inheritor of many great painters who preceded me and made tradition living, on-going and ever renewable like nature itself, by finding dynamic, contemporary and personal ways to depict and interpret *their* life and *their* time." This philosophy has guided Soyer's art for over forty years.

In the last year of the nineteenth century the town of Borisoglebsk in the government of Tambov, South Russia, was not an environment to foster art—a poverty-stricken, dreary town, typical of many in Czarist Russia. Here Raphael Soyer and his twin brother Moses were born on December 25, 1899, the first of six children of Abraham and Rebecca Schoar. The father was a teacher of Hebrew literature and history, who also wrote in Hebrew fairytales for children and short stories for adults. An idealist, optimistic and impractical, he was much beloved by his students. His wife, temperamentally opposite, was reserved and pessimistic, and inclined to melancholy. Life was hard for the growing family, and doubly hard because they were Jews.

Nevertheless the Schoar home was bursting with aspirations, literary and artistic. Raphael and Moses read everything in their father's library, juvenile and adult: Tolstoi, Turgenev, Dostoevski, Gogol; and in Russian translation, Dickens and Thackeray, *Tom Sawyer, Hiawatha.* Raphael knew *Uncle Tom's Cabin* almost by heart. They had two languages, Russian and Hebrew; and in addition their father's students coached them in various subjects, so that they learned some French and German.

Abraham Schoar was also a devotee of art. He decorated the walls of their house with postcards of Russian paintings; and "it was from him," Raphael says, "that we first heard the names of Rembrandt, Raphael, Michelangelo." And he himself drew, in a naive but lively manner, pictures of birds, flowers and animals, specializing in prancing horses. From his designs his wife embroidered linens in bright colors.

Encouraged by their parents, Raphael and Moses and even their brother Isaac, seven years younger, drew constantly, mostly copies of their father's works. Their pictures would be passed on by the parents and put up on the walls, thus stimulating sibling rivalry. Isaac soon caught up with his elders. "Everyone in the family aspired to be something," Raphael says. "The brothers were obsessed by childish dreams of becoming Rembrandts and Raphaels, whose works were as yet entirely unknown to them."

The Schoar home became a gathering place for Abraham's pupils and other young people. Such gatherings with their danger of liberal ideas were not welcomed by the Czarist police, especially if they centered around a Jew. In the fall of 1912 the governor of the province refused to renew Abraham Schoar's residence permit, which was tantamount to exile. Within a few weeks the family—father, mother and six children—were on their way to the United States.

They landed in Philadelphia, where they stayed with the mother's relatives while Abraham went to New York to find work as a teacher of Hebrew. The five older children were sent to public school, and as foreigners without English were all put in the same kindergarten class. Raphael and Moses were outraged; they were better educated than most American children their age, in Borisoglebsk they had been admitted to the "gymnasium." In a few months they moved on to New York, settling in a poor neighborhood in the Bronx. Admitted to public school, the twins at first clung sullenly to their Russian, and even when they learned English they found it hard to adjust to school. "We were happy only in the badly lighted and ill ventilated back room in our apartment which our mother had allocated to us," Moses recalled. "Here we [including Isaac] did our lessons, posed for one another, and painted and drew."

Nevertheless the two older boys went through grammar school in two years and at fifteen entered high school, where things were better. In the meantime Abraham Soyer, although he eked out his salary by writing for the Yiddish press, could not make both ends meet. Raphael and Moses helped with odd jobs; but finally they decided to leave school and go to work. For the next ten years or so Raphael was to work full-time or part-time, at all hours, on all kinds of jobs: among others, selling newspapers, tending soda fountains, and serving as an errand boy.

At the same time Raphael and Moses determined to study art seriously. They had already discovered the free evening drawing classes at Cooper Union, which Raphael attended for three years. In the fall of 1918, aged eighteen, they entered the free school of the National Academy of Design. But they were becoming increasingly aware, in Raphael's words, "of our special problem of being twins, of having the same interests and attitudes, which tended to make our work look alike." On Moses' initiative they decided to study in different art schools. Moses went to the Educational Alliance Art School on the lower East Side, where many future well-known artists received their first training. Among his fellow students were Peter Blume, Chaim Gross, Saul Berman and Louis Ribak.

Raphael continued at the Academy. Now adult, he was physically small (five feet two) and slight in build. Introspective, intensely shy, inarticulate, with a low, barely audible voice he compensated for his small stature by his will power and his quiet, almost desperate determination. In knowledge of art he was still entirely naive; almost his first sight of original paintings had been a visit to the Metropolitan Museum when he was sixteen. But he soon learned to paint from the model competently by academic standards,which meant photographic naturalism and clever brushwork. Sargent was held up as the example to follow; of any broader viewpoint, even the realism of the Henri group, nothing was said. Among his fellow students were a few non-conformists: Ben Shahn, Paul Cadmus, Sol Wilson and the future art historian Meyer Schapiro; but his shyness kept him from knowing them.

He remained at the Academy, in day life classes, for four school years, through the spring of 1922. For two months in the winter of 1920/21 he also studied at the Art Students League under Guy Pène du Bois, and in early 1923 he returned for three more months with du Bois. For the first time he had found a teacher with whom he was in rapport, and after leaving du Bois' class he would sometimes bring his paintings to the older artist's studio.

For about five years after leaving art school he worked at non-artistic jobs, painting in his spare time, at home. Continuing shyness kept him from social contacts outside his family. Moses, more sociable, brought home fellow students and friends. Appointed an instructor at the Alliance, in 1926 he was awarded a travelling fellowship, married one of his students, and set off for Europe. His class was taken over by Isaac, who in turn married and went to Paris in 1928. So Raphael was the last to leave home, to be married, and to go abroad.

"As soon as I left the Academy," Raphael wrote in 1946, "I made a conscious effort to forget everything I had learned there. . . . I started from the beginning again and painted in a frank and almost naive manner subjects of ordinary interest that were part of my immediate life." When he was about twenty-six he began to find himself as an artist. To that time belong several cityscapes: East Side streets and parks, children playing, old men sitting around, pushcart peddlers. These pictures have a simplicity and an absence of academic formulas that bear out his statement about forgetting the Academy's teachings; it is hard to believe that the man who painted them had studied there for four years. Everything is seen in terms of flat pattern, with little concern for naturalistic light. The drawing is almost childlike. Colors are subdued and pale. Pervaded by the sadness of mean streets on gray days, these scenes still have a touch of quiet lyricism.

His early figure paintings have similar qualities. *Dancing Lesson* shows his sister Rebecca teaching Moses, to the tune of a harmonica played by the youngest, Israel, while the parents look on, the mother under her rubberplant. This typical Bronx domestic scene has a definite element of humor, verging on caricature. It would be hard to say how much this was intentional or how much the result of naive candor. Twenty years later he wrote of his works of this time, "The altogether simple way in

THE MISSION.
c. 1935. Lithograph. 12⅛ x 17⅝.
Whitney Museum of American Art.

which these pictures were painted gave them a humorous aspect which was not intended"; but one wonders. In any case, it is a gentle humor. Here too the style is flat and without chiaroscuro. But the light cool color scheme with its delicate grays reveals an innate chromatic sense—that gift which, like poetry, must be inborn.

The same candor governs his early portraits of his father and mother; even those nearest to him were not flattered in any way. The main concern was truth of character. *Nude* (the first he had painted since art school) has a similar honesty; this scrawny female is completely devoid of glamor, yet touching in her naked humanity, like an Eve by some Flemish primitive.

This was a period of primitivism among certain young American painters, influenced by the Douanier Rousseau. With them it was far from naive; all of them knew better. Soyer's early primitivism seems more genuine, the result of his urge to paint the things he knew best in a purely personal style. But this simplistic phase did not last long. As he wrote in 1946: "Encouraged by a number of friends, I could have . . . remained a permanent 'primitive.' But my eagerness to learn my craft and to widen the content of my paintings prevented me." Within a year of *Dancing Lesson* he was producing a work as relatively skillful as *Susan*. And when we come to the figure pieces of 1929, all primitivism has vanished. Forms are roundly modelled, with a deft touch; and light and shadow have become important elements. The style is precise and sharp-edged, the color light and cool.

Soyer exhibited for the first time in 1926 with the Salons of America. There his work was seen by Alexander Brook, only a year and half older but already with a growing reputation, and a position as assistant director of the Whitney Studio Club.

LAUNDRESS.
1941-42. Lithograph. 14½ x 10¾.

Brook helped to sell a painting, and introduced him to the Club, then the liveliest center anywhere for young and liberal artists. From early 1927 Soyer was included in all the members' exhibitions, until the Club was disbanded in the fall of 1928. Often he would take a new painting to Juliana Force, director of the Club and of its successor the Whitney Studio Galleries, and she would buy it for the price he asked—modest enough, between $150 and $300. By 1931 Mrs. Force had bought five paintings and a drawing, all of which were included in the collection of the Whitney Museum when it opened that fall. Next year the museum bought a sixth painting, the first institution to purchase his work. Thenceforth he was included in almost all the Whitney's annual and biennial exhibitions.

In 1928 he took a painting to the Daniel Gallery, the most active dealer handling younger Americans. Charles Daniel said, "When you have twelve such pictures, we will give you a one-man exhibition." It took him a year to paint them in his spare time, and his first one-man show opened in April 1929. The reviews were favorable, two or three pictures were sold, and Daniel added him to his list of artists.

Soyer now felt that he was a real painter. He gave up outside jobs, stopped working at home, and rented studio space, at first shared with other young artists, then entirely his own—all on the lower East Side. The process of leaving home, which for him had been late and prolonged, was ending. And on February 8, 1931, he married Rebecca Letz, a school friend of his sister Fanny, and like her a teacher.

In every way his life was expanding in these years. His work showed a steady gain in sophistication. His cityscapes were now constructed in three dimensions, with a fine precision, as in the skillfully drawn curve of the bridge in *Under the Bridge,* subtly distorted so that it leads back into the picture; a piece of draftsmanship that convinced the critic Henry McBride that the painter "could not be amateurish any more." The flat grayness of early city scenes was replaced by observed sunlight and shadow, and his color range broadened, sometimes reaching an almost impressionistic pitch.

Similar gains took place in his figure paintings. The 1930's saw a series of intimate interiors, centered around women, shown singly or by twos or threes, conversing, resting, sleeping, or simply existing. The pervading mood was one of quietness and introspection. The impassive faces show no signs of *joie de vivre;* rather, a meditative brooding, sometimes a strain of melancholy. Only occasionally does a man appear with a woman, but he remains subordinate, and there seems little affirmative relation between them; she plays solitaire while he lies on the bed, his back turned. On the other hand, the relationship of woman to woman always appears close.

These young women have no conventional glamor. Far from *soignées,* they sit or lie on couches or disorderly beds, informally dressed or half-dressed, cigarette in hand, with frowsy unkempt hair. Yet there is an undertone of muted sensuousness. Sometimes they appear in dishabille, revealing deeply cleft breasts, bare thighs. One is always conscious of the body beneath the clothes, and that the clothes may come off at any minute; indeed, the models are often beginning to undress.

Unhackneyed observation of natural attitudes and gestures marks these paintings; the women seem unposed, unaware of being painted. One thinks of Degas; as Soyer later wrote, "At this time I became fascinated by the art of Degas—worldly, analytical, refined, the antithesis of anything naive." But the element of exposé in Degas' depiction of women bathing is not present in Soyer's attitude; his women are seen with warmth and intimacy, and a note of sentiment. There is nothing of the *voyeur* in him. One feels that these women must somehow be close to him; not the usual professional models but friends, women he knew well. Many of them, in fact, were persons interesting in themselves: dancers, actresses, artists, citizens of Manhattan's unfashionable Bohemia, the lower East Side.

Each woman is an individual. Soyer's feeling for character has always been sensitive and true, capturing the subtle differences of shape and contour that make the person an individual like no one else. There is none of the standardization of features that marks the academic portraitist and figure painter. Indeed his eye for character often carried him beyond the limits of objective realism into a free, plastic accentuation of physical idiosyncrasies.

These figure paintings show a decisive maturing of style. No longer sharp-edged, forms are bathed in light and air. Light has become a major factor, revealing and modelling forms, casting deep shadows, and creating a general twilit tonality out of which the strongly lighted central forms—faces, hands, bodies—emerge with a vivid immediacy. The magic of light simplifies, suppresses details, unites all elements. The color is low-toned, with blacks, warm browns, fine grays, and only infrequent more brilliant notes. A sensuous pleasure in the handling of pigment is manifest. In many respects his style was related to certain other young painters of the time, especially Brook, Kuniyoshi, and Bouché, who were all friends of the cosmopolitan Jules Pascin and bore the impress of his magnetic personality. Soyer never met Pascin; he had a date to do so, but at the last moment his diffidence got the better of him. But Pascin's influence was evident in Soyer's paintings of the time, and even more in his drawings.

These were the years of the Depression. It had little financial effect on Soyer, since he had nothing to lose. But it affected him in other ways. With his background he was naturally to the left in his political beliefs. Soon after the John Reed Club was founded in 1929 he became a member, attended meetings, and joined in painting collective social protest murals, signed "John Reed Club." Here he met Diego Rivera and was much impressed by him, and when his murals in Rockefeller Center were destroyed, Soyer took part in the artists' demonstrations outside the building. When the Club started an art school he was invited to teach (without pay), thus beginning his long teaching career. He was a signer of the 1936 call for the American Artists Congress and became a member of the resulting organization, serving on several committees, including the national executive committee.

These interests found expression in a new type of subject: life in the poor sections of New York. The city as subject-matter had been discovered thirty years before by the Henri group, who had pictured it with robust realism, but without dwelling on its aspects of poverty and squalor. Even the brilliant realist George Bellows had seen tenement life as a picturesque spectacle. But with the Depression came a younger generation who looked at the city with more critical eyes: the slums, the unemployed, the submerged life of the Bowery, the tawdriness of the city's glamor. Their basic motivation was still affirmative love of the city, but their realism was more drastic. Some of them—Reginald Marsh, Katherine Schmidt, Isabel Bishop, Edward Laning—had been pupils of Kenneth Hayes Miller, who combined the subject-matter of Fourteenth Street with classic concepts of design.

Soyer did not need the Depression to make him aware of the facts of life in most of New York; he had lived with them since childhood. As boy and youth he had roamed the streets, drawing the people of the East Side. About 1933 he embarked on a series of paintings and prints of life on the Bowery and Fourteenth Street, focussing on the derelicts—men existing without hope, begging, sleeping in parks and under bridges, dependent on missions for food and shelter. Three bums on benches in Union Square, one asleep, the others looking lost, while in the background the Father of His Country rides his bronze horse. Homeless transients sitting in a flophouse waiting patiently for sleeping space. Five men, old and young, being fed in a mission, under a sign: "HOW LONG SINCE YOU WROTE TO MOTHER?"

In spite of Soyer's political beliefs, these works contain no propaganda. This was the heyday of the social protest school with its doctrine that art must express a social viewpoint (Marxist, naturally) to be valid. Many of Soyer's friends subscribed to this creed. But only twice did he paint pictures with any social message, and they were not among his successes. His portrayal of the underprivileged was objective. But a deep sympathy for human misery was apparent. This identification with suffering, expressed in objective terms, recalls his early admiration for the realism of the great Russian writers. These pictures revealed fully his love of human character in whatever form it could be found—in the gaunt, beat-up faces, toothless, eroded by hunger and exposure and cheap alcohol, in the starved bodies under the misfitting clothes.

Soyer's bums were not products of his imagination. Showing an interviewer in 1934 a picture of men sleeping under the arches of Williamsburg Bridge, he remarked, "They did not mind when I sketched them. I knew most of them." That this was so is proved by the way certain faces reappear: dead-beats whom he got to pose for him in his studio, often giving them not only money but a night's lodging. The most familiar face is that of Walter Broe. One day Soyer noticed an old man fishing through a subway grating, using a long pole with chewing gum on the end, to pick up small coins dropped by careless people—a form of gainful occupation

YASUO KUNIYOSHI.

1941. Ink and watercolor. 10 x 8.
Nebraska Art Association.

REBECCA.

1931. Ink and watercolor. 9½ x 7.

STUDIES OF GIRL PULLING UP SLIP.

1961. Pencil and watercolor. 23½ x 15½.
Collection of Mr. and Mrs. Samuel Shore.

prevalent during the Depression. One look at Broe's face showed Soyer that he had found the perfect model—a thin haggard face with watchful anxious eyes under a worried forehead; a face that had been through much, that could express dejection, hope, humbleness, skepticism, humor; a face as unforgetable as any in the history of painting. Thenceforth Broe appeared in almost all Soyer's East Side pictures: as a principal actor *(Reading from Left to Right),* in a group of his fellows *(Transients),* or as a bystander *(Office Girls).* Soyer introduced him to other artists, and Mr. Broe, as he was usually called, became a favorite model for the painters of Fourteenth Street, especially Marsh, Katherine Schmidt and Isabel Bishop.

Soyer's Bowery paintings, direct out of reality, owed little to other art. Each man was specifically characterized, from his face to the patches on his clothes. First-hand visual observation produced *In the City Park,* with its figures in the immediate foreground, their faces lit by strong warm light, seen against the darkening park—an utterly authentic visual document. The somber tonality of these canvases was appropriate to their subjects. Soyer wrote later: "When I discovered the joy of being able to represent accurately and in full detail all those men on park benches and in missions, their faces, gestures, and the wrinkles of their skin and coats, I became aware of the danger of naturalism. . . . I do not regret that period however because I learned much then." How much he learned is shown by his growing artistry as the series developed. Compared to *In the City Park,* with all its honest virtues, *Reading from Left to Right* is more freely and fluidly executed, from the masterly characterization of the men to the beautiful calligraphy of the hand-lettered sign. The earlier work had included more complex forms in deep space, not completely integrated; whereas the later one concentrated on fewer elements finely realized, with all the forms contained within the picture plane.

In the middle 1930's Soyer attacked a different kind of street scene, peopling the sidewalks with crowds of women: shop girls, office girls, shoppers. The locale was not the Bowery, but neither was it Fifth Avenue; it was still around Union Square, and the women were working girls and housewives, not the fashionable. And in the background was usually a bum or two. Women walking, greeting, talking, window shopping; office girls out to lunch; boisterous shop girls released from behind the counter. These works were not satirical, and carried no message for or against the social order. They were motivated by love of the changing spectacle of the streets, by pleasure in the myriad variations in faces and bodies, hats and clothes, and above all by absorption in womankind, her occupations, actions and gestures. Each woman in the crowd is an individual; for example, the thin, rather homely and hungry-looking girl gazing out at us from *Office Girls*—an appealing face, as distinctive as Mr. Broe's next to her. Soyer's crowds are always composed of individuals, not of featureless robots. His street scenes carry that conviction of coming directly out of the common life that marks good genre art of all time. They show a new attention to outdoor light. The varicolored dresses and hats, seen in full daylight, create an interplay of color and light and shadow that adds to the sense of movement and life. Among Soyer's contemporaries these crowd scenes were closest to Marsh's, but without the latter's tumultuous mass movement or satire; nor did they embody the Renaissance concepts of form that marked Miller's ex-students. They were more naturalistic and more purely visual.

Nevertheless they show a growing concern with problems of design. This is apparent in the two versions of *Bus Passengers;* in the second the design was strengthened by moving the stout woman to the center, where she forms a solid pivot for a more centralized composition. Still more deliberately composed was *Waiting Room,* his largest and most ambitious painting so far. The drab theme of people sitting and waiting fascinated him, as it did Isabel Bishop: the variety of human beings, and their moods of weariness, impatience or resignation. Related to this theme was a series during World War II of soldiers in Pennsylvania Station saying goodbye to their wives, mothers and sweethearts. These were practically the only reflection of the war in his paintings, proving again how a-political his art was.

Once launched on his career, Soyer had been fortunate. After the Daniel Gallery closed in 1931, a victim of the Depression, he took four paintings around to other dealers. Some offered to take them on consignment, but he needed money. When he finally came to the Valentine Gallery, then one of the most "in", specializing in the Ecole de Paris, Valentine Dudensing bought all four pictures on the spot, became his dealer, and gave him three one-man shows during the 1930's. After that Soyer switched to the Associated American Artists, who in their impressive new duplex gallery, with a stable of artists that included Benton, Wood, Curry and Grosz, were temporarily making other dealers look small. In 1941 the gallery held a big one-man exhibition, with sixty paintings, and two more shows in the 1940's.

From the early 1930's he was represented regularly in the large annual and biennial exhibitions of American art. As early as 1932 he received the Kohnstamm Prize at the Art Institute of Chicago, and thereafter a succession of awards for two decades, including the prestigious Temple Medal of the Pennsylvania Academy and the First Clark Prize of the Corcoran Gallery. The critics were almost unanimously favorable from his first one-man show on, including reviewers of all persuasions, from social realists like Jerome Klein to the conservative Royal Cortissoz, who in 1938 called him "one of the small group of first-rate painters this country boasts of at present."

In the meantime, Soyer had been pursuing a parallel career, printmaking. He had started early to make prints, at first in etching, then lithography. His first lithographs had been executed on transfer paper, but in 1933 he began to draw directly on stone. The medium, which permits building the picture primarily in tone, without dependence on pure line, has proved particularly suited to his pictorial style. In his lithographs as in his paintings, a dominant role is played by light, which models the forms roundly, with strong contrasts of lighted surfaces and deep shadows, and in between, a wide range of finely modulated grays, achieved by a complex technique of working into the darks by scratching down to the white surface. But underneath the tonal network is always a solid structure of draftsmanship. Some of his prints are based on paintings, others are new conceptions. In either case, they are as completely realized as his works in any medium. Altogether, the volume and the quality of his prints have established him as one of our leading printmakers.

With the years Soyer's youthful shyness disappeared, and he acquired many friends among fellow artists. They were by no means confined to those who shared his artistic viewpoint; among his best friends, for example, was Arshile Gorky. He particularly liked to paint and draw portraits of them, and of older artists whom he admired. By 1941 he had accumulated enough to include in his one-man show a section of twenty-three works, called "My Contemporaries and Elders." Among them were Sloan, Stella, Hartley, Walkowitz, Burliuk, Gorky, Marsh, Gropper, Evergood, Avery, and his own brother Moses. Products of affection and admiration, these artist portraits had a special flavor quite unlike the usual commissioned work. One of his closest friends, and his favorite artist model, was David Burliuk, that unique figure in our art—a genuine naive, an artist of the purest, most innocent poetry. Soyer portrayed him many times, always absorbed in his beloved art of painting. The series of individual likenesses culminated in *My Friends,* his largest canvas so far and the second largest he has ever done, representing his studio, with Nicolai Cikovsky, Moses Soyer, Burliuk and Chaim Gross, and in the background, his back turned, Raphael at his easel. A scroll in the foreground reads: "Friendship is the wine of life."

From the beginning of his career his most frequent model has been himself. He has painted and drawn literally scores of self portraits; probably not even he knows how many, but they must number close to Rembrandt's sixty-two. His is a highly paintable face, and he pictures it without self-flattery. It is interesting to trace the changes from the young man in his twenties who inscribed the portrait in the Phillips Collection, "Raphael Soyer, New York artist, who is sleepy when he is not painting," to the mature, experienced painter who now gazes out at us—always brush in hand. Several pictures are complete studio interiors, with himself and his model. And in many crowd scenes one can spot him somewhere in the background.

About the time he turned forty a change came over Soyer's subjects. The city scenes stopped, except for a few like *Subway Platform,* with only two figures. For more than a decade his art remained indoors. The paintings of single figures of women continued and increased. The few men were mostly fellow artists. His special sensitivity to women, his absorption in them as both human beings and physical presences, grew during these years. As always, they were individuals, sometimes definite personages such as Maureen Stapleton, more often friends, or profes-

Standing Figure, (Back
1964. Pencil and
watercolor. 17 x 13.
Collection of S. J. Gross.

sional models, who often became friends. Some were young and attractive, for he never avoided physical beauty. But attractive or homely, his main concern was the separate private person, and her identity as a unique human being. In some the psychological content was intensified. Often these women seem troubled personalities, who were drawn to him by the quality of sympathetic understanding they felt in him. His awareness of this was evident in his portrayals of them: lonely figures sitting, eyes downcast or gazing into space, hands tightly clasped, haunted faces withdrawn into their subjective worlds.

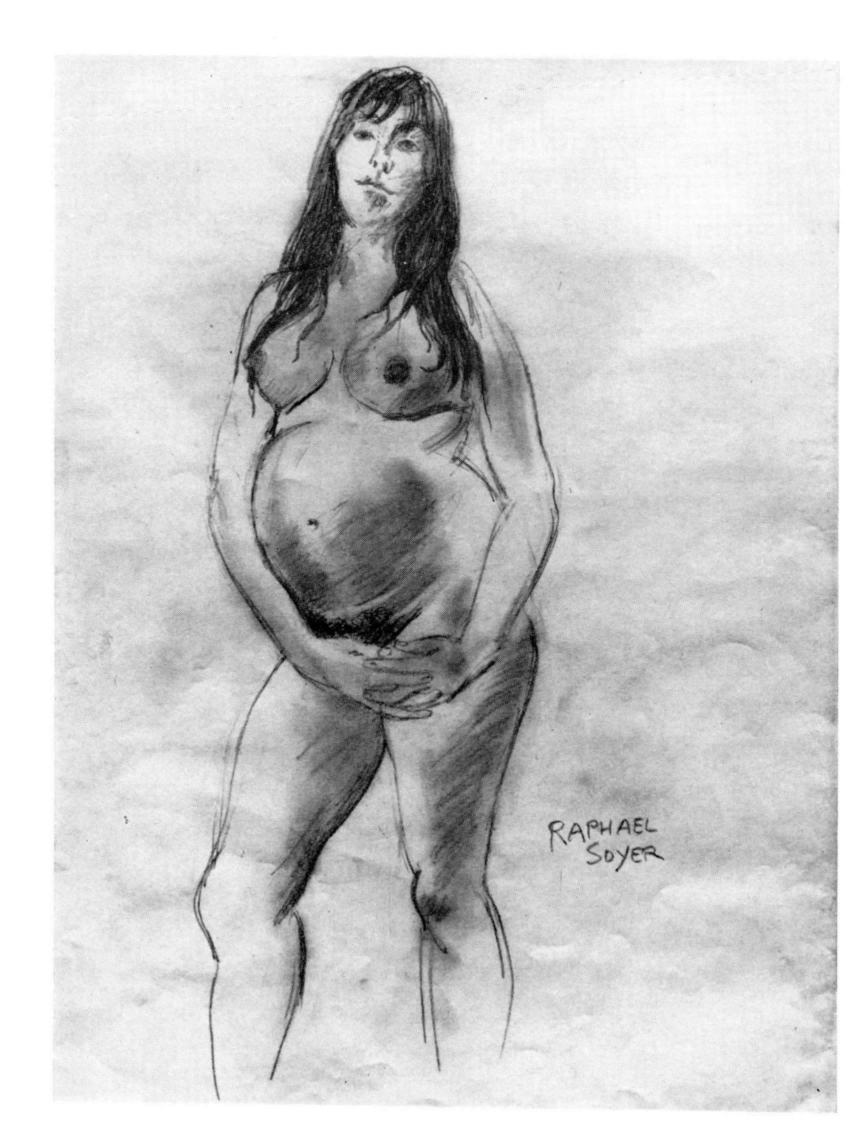

PREGNANT WOMAN.
c. 1964. Pencil.
16⅞ x 13⅞.

This psychological element was combined with sensuous realization of the woman as a physical being: the fineness of the female body, its amplitude of form and its flowing lines. From student days he had constantly drawn the nude, and his many drawings showed a franker sensuousness than his paintings of the time, delighting in picturing the body in every kind of position, in realizing to the full its forms and rhythms. These years of observation and drawing resulted in a sure grasp of bodily structure and movement, and in command of a line that was strong, precise, and finely modulated. For an artist who is so painterly, this linear clarity and strength are unusual. But he has always thought of his drawings (often heightened with watercolor) as a special category of his work, not directly related to his paintings but independent works of art.

Soyer loves to paint and draw pregnant women. How he manages to secure all these pregnant models is a mystery. And they are not just in the first months; these are unmistakable fully-developed pregnancies. (In at least one case he is reputed to have kept a model until the day before delivery.) His feeling for the body of a woman carrying a child is something special—a tenderness, an admiration. And it does not matter whether the pregnancy is legitimate; often it is not, in the amoral circles from which some of his models come. His full-length *Nude* (page 55) is an extraordinary achievement, such as few present-day painters have attempted. One notes the touching contrast between the full belly and the awkward legs and feet, which seem hardly able to support the body. The ungainliness of pregnancy is never minimized.

Women's occupations played an increasing part in his subjects. The art of dancing, especially modern dance, had always attracted him. Of *Fé Alf and Her Pupils* he wrote that "it was done when modern dancing was at the height of its 'Renaissance period.' I was particularly interested in the dancers, many of whom I knew personally, and often visited their studios to watch them work. Fé Alf with her tall, commanding and beautifully strong figure was especially interesting to paint." It is significant that the dancers were almost always shown at rest, or putting on their leotards, and that he seldom showed them in action—a problem of translating physical motion into painting, which he evidently wisely concluded was not his *métier*.

On a humbler level were dressmakers, an occupation that interested him so much that it brought forth a whole series of paintings. In all these representations of women at work a new feature was their physical environment. Instead of existing in undefined space, they were in specific interiors. And the play of interior light, often from more than one source, introduced another element. All these factors produced more complexity in both subjects and design. In design it was an enrichment; in place of a few central forms, the whole interior space and the objects in it were part of the composition. At first the interior was little more than a background, but soon the shape of the room, the relations of figures and objects to it and to one another, assumed almost as much importance as the figures themselves. Windows played a part, not only for the light they transmitted but as components of design. In works such as *Girl in a Brown Jacket* windows and walls create rectangular patterns against which the figures are silhouetted. There is a growing feeling for the balance of masses, of light and dark areas, and for the interrelations of straight and curvilinear lines. Screens are used as intermediate planes between the foreground figures and the further walls. In *The Screen* an effective composition is built out of nothing more than a three-fold screen with brilliant-colored clothes hanging on it in strong light—simply a few planes, and space and light. Containing walls, instead of being at right angles to the eye, are slanted at varying angles to create a design of oblique planes surrounding the central forms.

The gain in his sense of design is apparent by comparison of *Dressmaker's Shop* with *Seamstresses* of about four years later. The former, with its fine relation of the interior to the figures, is still a composition primarily of horizontals and verticals. In the later painting the oblique angles of floor and walls are more interesting than the rectangular grid of the earlier work; and the principal forms are larger, filling the whole space, and the interplay of their curved and straight lines creates dynamic design. This growth in his control of three-dimensional design was the major development of his work of this middle period.

His color was still relatively subdued, running a gamut of grays and grayed hues and earthy colors. Flesh tones were not rosy or pearly but muted gray-gold. Color schemes were simplified to a few main tones. But within these limits he showed a highly developed sense of color relations, achieving harmonies that were sometimes subtle and delicate, sometimes rich and full-bodied. Color was always closely integrated with form, coming forward or retreating, helping to build form and space.

In the American art world as a whole, these years—the late 1940's and early 1950's—saw the rise of abstract art as a dominant movement. Soyer had always believed completely in representational art. "I consider art as a means of communication as well as a vehicle for self-expression," he wrote. "The content of my art is people—men, women and children . . . within their daily setting. . . . *I choose to be a realist and a humanist in art.*" With these beliefs, he naturally was strongly opposed to abstraction. Like other representational artists he felt that the powers-that-be in the art world—museums, critics, dealers—had gone overboard for abstraction and were ignoring all other viewpoints.

In the spring of 1950 he decided to do something about it, and wrote postcards to a number of representational painters suggesting that they get together to consider the state of the art world. In response about ten painters met in an Italian restaurant in New York. "We found it very pleasant to sit around a table and talk about what we believed in," wrote one of them, Henry Varnum Poor. They met again, and the group grew. Finally they decided to assemble their opinions in a small annual to be called *Reality.* The first issue in 1953 opened with a statement of common beliefs signed by forty-seven artists, including many eminent names.

Reality brought reactions much wider than its sponsors expected. From advanced circles came denials of over-emphasis on abstraction, and accusations of "McCarthyism." But from artists all over the country came so many letters of support that the editors were swamped, and another printing of the magazine had to be made. Second and third annual issues in 1954 and 1955 contained highly interesting and contentious statements by leading representational artists. Soyer was on the editorial board, the mailing address was his studio, and all the material passed through his hands. In perspective, *Reality* makes good reading, and one wishes that it could have continued.

With the dominance of advanced trends Soyer's reputation like that of fellow traditionalists suffered a partial eclipse. His work was now shown only occasionally in the large national exhibitions, except in institutions where comprehensive policies were continued, such as the Pennsylvania Academy and the Whitney Museum. On the other hand, he exhibited regularly at the National Academy, and in 1949 was elected an Associate and two years later an Academician; and honors came from the American Academy of Arts and Letters and the National Institute of Arts and Letters. He continued to have one-man shows, and strangely enough the critical reception remained cordial, even from those of whom this would not be expected. And his sales never suffered; indeed they increased, and he commanded higher prices.

A notable fact in Soyer's development is that while many traditionalists have either gone over to advanced art, given up in discouragement or fallen into a rut, his art has grown with the years. In the late 1950's came a major breakthrough: fresh subjects and new attitudes toward them, greater complexity, larger scale, freer handling, and in particular a basic expansion in color.

The first fruit of this change was *Farewell to Lincoln Square,* his second largest painting so far. Along with other artists he had been forced to give up his studio in the old Lincoln Arcade Building which was about to be demolished to make way for Lincoln Center. The group of fellow tenants is leaving the Square, Raphael himself in the background waving goodbye, with Rebecca beside him. The farewell mood is evident in the downcast look of the young woman in the foreground and the anxious expression of her companion. With the dominant central figure, supported by those behind her, this is one of his strongest, most concentrated designs. In color it is in striking contrast to any previous work. The relatively dark tonality has been replaced by a much lighter, purer and cooler palette. The clothes of the two leading women have brilliant colors that had not appeared before: emerald green, ultramarine blue, violet, cool scarlet. And for the first time the positive colors are juxtaposed, not separated by neutral tones. Grays have by no means been abandoned; the general ground is made up of warm grays that accentuate the vividness of the stronger colors, and unify the whole tonality. The technique has a new complexity, with translucent glazes contrasting with heavier passages. The handling, at once sure and delicate, gives life to the whole surface, so that the canvas rewards close study.

When I recently asked Soyer how he accounts for this increased freedom of color and technique, he said, "Color is something that comes with age. When an artist is young he is concerned with representing things accurately, but as he grows older he becomes freer." His present freedom is the ripeness that results from long experience. For him it involves no loss in directness and freshness of vision; on the contrary, his recent work is fresher than ever in visual sensation.

Another cause is undoubtedly his continuing practice of almost daily working from the model. In recent years he has painted the nude more than ever before. Many of these canvases are small and sketchy, seeming like exercises for the eye and hand. Others are complete compositions that demonstrate his new freedom of approach. In *Melancholia II,* for example, we have the perennial theme of a woman and a bed, but treated quite differently from earlier versions. The psychological content is similar: a woman caught off guard, whose slumped attitude, troubled eyes, limp hands and unkempt hair denote anxiety and disorientation. But by contrast this is one of his most ingratiating works in color. The room is bathed in light, without the dark shadows of earlier works. Flesh is no longer sallow but alive with varied hues. The clear, radiant color is close to the impressionist palette, as is the

RESTLESS NUDE.
1966. Pencil. 13½ x 16½.

BLACK STOCKINGS.

1966. Pencil and watercolor. 21¾ x 15½.
Collection of Mr. and Mrs. Albert J. Dreitzer.

technique of divided tones. With all its seeming casualness, the picture is composed with the art that conceals art. Everything is at irregular angles; floor, walls and screen are unrectangular; even the bed is twisted. There are no right angles, no pure verticals or horizontals, no lines parallel to the four edges of the picture, and no planes parallel to the surface of the canvas. The play of diagonal lines at subtly varying angles creates one of his most personal and satisfying designs.

One factor in Soyer's recent development may be his travels abroad in recent years. He had first returned to Europe in 1935, but at that time he felt "lost" and was glad to get back to New York. Twenty-four years passed before he and Rebecca went abroad again, but beginning in 1959 they have made five visits of around three months each, going to the principal cities of thirteen or fourteen countries. These have not been sightseeing trips; every possible moment has been spent in museums, where Raphael has studied the paintings with passionate intensity, and made drawings of details from them. These travels are recorded in two books, *A Painter's Pilgrimage* and *Homage to Thomas Eakins, Etc.,* with a third just finished. Illustrated with his drawings, these books have the special attraction of an artist's insights into the art he loves. The range of his interest is very wide, but his greatest devotion is given to the supreme masters of the sixteenth and seventeenth centuries, and above all, Rembrandt.

In American art Soyer's highest admiration has long been for Thomas Eakins. After the big Eakins exhibition in 1961 and 1962, he resolved to embody his admiration in his largest painting, *Homage to Thomas Eakins.* The precedent was Fantin-Latour's *Hommage à Delacroix,* and the criterion for inclusion was the individual's respect for Eakins, not any direct relationship. The preliminary selection of five or six artists, plus myself as Eakins' biographer, was eventually expanded to eleven. Soyer painted separate portraits of each of us, except Marsh, for whom he used one done in 1941. At one point he told me that he did not intend to include himself, but I pointed out that every painter of a homage had done so. In the end he placed Moses in the center of the front row, while he himself appears inconspicuously in the left background, with his daughter Mary behind him, bringing in a tray of drinks. The others, reading from left to right, are Leonard Baskin, Edward Hopper, myself, Reginald Marsh, Jack Levine, John Koch, Edwin Dickinson, Henry Varnum Poor and John Dobbs. Behind us is Eakins' great *Gross Clinic,* with *Salutat* at the left and the 1908 *William Rush* at the right. What with getting the sitters to pose, planning the whole composition, and then executing it, the project extended over two and a half years. Even before the big picture was finished, that fast-moving collector Joseph H. Hirshhorn had bought it and all the studies for it.

In the late 1950's and the 1960's the Soyers lived on Second Avenue, in the heart of the East Village, which had supplanted Greenwich Village as New York's avant-garde artistic and literary center. Here Soyer painted one of his largest and most complex canvases, *Village East Street Scene.* "It is the result of my seven years' living and working on lower Second Avenue," he writes. "I became acquainted with some of the artists and writers. I tried to get the feeling of that area, the bearded, long-haired young men, the loose-haired, blue-jeaned girls with ecstatic faces, white mothers with Negro babies—on the background of drab walls bearing Fall-out Shelter signs above indecent and sentimental scribblings, barrages of green and red lights, and arrowed one-way street signs. I wanted to convey a feeling of energy and life in an atmosphere of deprivation and drabness. Like *Homage to Thomas Eakins,* it's a painting composed of portraits, some of them well-known, for example, the poets Allen Ginsberg, Gregory Corso, Diane di Prima." Of Ginsberg's and Corso's poetry he said, "I know little about poetry, but I like these compassionate, blasphemous, hallucinatory, self-revealing poems. . . . Is this kind of poetry analogous to avant-garde painting which also claims to mirror our confused, unhappy times? If so, the poetry makes more sense to me."

He was particularly interested in Diane di Prima, who had posed for him some years earlier, and he made her the leading character in the composition, a somnambulistic figure walking with raised face and vision-seeing eyes. Behind her are Ginsberg and Corso, and in the left background the playwright LeRoi Jones. In this latest street scene as in those of the late 1930's, Soyer has made a crowd out of a few individuals, and has captured the life and movement of city streets. But there is a new element: today's atmosphere of tension and restlessness, of rebellion and rejection. It is embodied not only in the faces and bodies and clothes, portrayed with such particularity, but in the off-beat unbalanced design with its center at the extreme left, so that the principals seem to be walking through and out of the picture. And a similar mood is expressed in the color, a ground of varying hues of leaden gray out of which the positive notes emerge with a flickering flamelike intensity. The brushwork throughout is rich and highly sensitive, charged with a nervous vitality that makes every inch of the surface alive.

In his most recent painting, which he calls *Á Watteau,* Soyer has carried his fascination with contemporary revolt a step further, into the hipster world. The sight of a be-in in Central Park reminded him of Watteau's scenes from the *théâtre français,* and specifically *Gilles* in the Louvre, on which his painting is based. "This is a picture of what can often be seen these days in Central Park," he writes, "groups of friendly young people playing musical instruments, beating drums, clapping out rhythms with their hands. The central figure is that of a rapt-expressioned girl holding a daffodil in one hand, the other raised, open-palmed. She may be symbolic, if you will, of peace, youth, goodwill, friendship." In his acceptance of these latest way-out manifestations of our times, and in the freshness of his interpretation of them, Soyer at sixty-seven shows himself not only more skilled in eye and hand, but younger in heart, than he was in the grim 1930's.

BIOGRAPHICAL NOTE

Raphael Soyer and his twin brother Moses were born on December 25, 1899, in Borisoglebsk, Government of Tambov, Russia. They were the first of six children of Abraham and Bella Schneyer Schoar. Their father was a teacher of Hebrew literature and history. Raphael and Moses attended local schools and were also taught by their father and his pupils. From early childhood they and their younger brother Isaac drew constantly, encouraged by their parents. Because their home became a center for Abraham Schoar's students, the family was ordered to leave Russia, and left for the United States in 1912. They landed in Philadelphia and stayed there a few months, then moved to New York, settling in the Bronx.

Raphael and Moses went through public grammar school in two years, and entered Morris High School, continuing to draw and paint at home, and also studying drawing in Cooper Union at night; in Raphael's case, for three years, fall 1914 to spring 1917. But because of the family's financial situation the boys left high school and went to work. They also undertook serious study of art. Raphael entered the National Academy of Design school in the fall of 1918, at first in the "Life on Probation" class, then from January 1920 in the "Life in Full" class. His teacher for the first season was George W. Maynard, succeeded by Charles C. Curran. He remained at the Academy four seasons, through the spring of 1922. He also studied at the Art Students League of New York under Guy Pène du Bois for two months, December 1920 and January 1921, and later for three months, January through March 1923. In January 1926 he returned to the League for a month with Boardman Robinson.

After leaving the Academy he worked at various jobs, painting at home in his spare time. He exhibited first in 1926 in the Salons of America, where Alexander Brook saw his work and helped sell a picture. Brook introduced him to the Whitney Studio Club, and from early 1927 he exhibited in the Club's shows. In the next few years the Club's Director, Juliana Force, bought five of his paintings.

His first one-man show, at the Daniel Gallery in 1929, was well received by critics, and several paintings were sold; so he was able to give up outside jobs and paint full-time. On February 8, 1931, he married Rebecca Letz. They have a daughter, Mary (now Mrs. Arnold Lieber) and two grandsons, David and Joseph.

Beginning in the early 1930's he showed fairly regularly in the large annual and biennial American exhibitions of the Whitney Museum, the Carnegie Institute, the Art Institute of Chicago, the Corcoran Gallery of Art, the National Academy of Design, and the Pennsylvania Academy of the Fine Arts. He also had a series of one-man shows in New York galleries. His first award, in 1932, was followed by a number of others. He worked in the Graphic Arts Division of the WPA Federal Art Project in the 1930's, and in 1939 he and Moses painted two murals for the Kingsessing, Pa., Postal Station.

He has been a member of the American Society of Painters, Sculptors and Gravers, An American Group, Inc., the American Artists Congress, and Artists Equity Association. In 1949 he was elected an Associate of the National Academy of Design, and in 1951 an Academician. The National Institute of Arts and Letters, which had given him a Grant in Art in 1945, elected him a member in 1958.

His teaching career began about 1930 at the John

Reed Club, New York. He taught at the Art Students League in the 1933-34 session, and again from September 1935 through May 1942; at the American Artists School for several years after World War II; at the New School for Social Research from the fall of 1957 through 1962, sharing classes with Julian Levi and Camilo Egas, and with a class of his own; and at the National Academy for two seasons, 1965-67.

New York City has been his home since childhood. A few summer months in the late 1920's and early 1930's were spent in Gloucester, Provincetown and Ogunquit. From 1941 to 1948 the Soyers spent summers in Croton-on-Hudson, from 1949 to 1954 in Southampton, and since 1957 in Vinalhaven, Maine, except when they were abroad.

Raphael Soyer first returned to Europe in the summer of 1935 for about three months, visiting Paris, London, and the Soviet Union, then going with Rebecca to Belgium and Spain. From 1959 on the Soyers made five summer visits of about three months each to Europe, always including Paris and usually London, but also travelling widely on the Continent: in 1959 to Holland and Italy; in 1961 to Munich and Vienna, and for five weeks in Italy, two in Holland and one in Belgium; in 1963 to Italy, Germany, Vienna, the Soviet Union, and Holland; in 1964 to Spain and Italy; and in 1966 to the Scandinavian countries, Germany, Vienna, Italy and Holland. These travels, and the works of art studied, have resulted in two books, *A Painter's Pilgrimage* and *Homage to Thomas Eakins, Etc.*, with a third in preparation.

One-man exhibitions (all in New York): Daniel Gallery, April 1929. L'Elan Gallery, February 1932. Valentine Gallery, February 1933, February 1935, and February 1938. Macbeth Gallery, March 1935 (lithograph and drawings). Rehn Gallery, April 1939, with Peggy Bacon (small paintings, lithographs and drawings). Associated American Artists Galleries, March 1941, March 1948, and March 1953. Weyhe Gallery, March 1944 (drawings). Babcock Galleries, December 1956 (drawings). Krasner Gallery, November 1957 (drawings). ACA Gallery, November 1960. Alfredo Valente Gallery, November 1961 (drawings and watercolors). Forum Gallery, April 1964, with Joseph Hirsch and Joseph Floch (drawings). Forum Gallery, April 1966. Whitney Museum of American Art, Retrospective Exhibition, October 25 to December 3, 1967, subsequently shown in six other American museums.

Awards: Art Institute of Chicago, October 1932, M. V. Kohnstamm Prize of $250, for *Subway.* Pennsylvania Academy of the Fine Arts, January 1934, Carol H. Beck Gold Medal for Best Portrait in Oil, for *Gittel.* Carnegie International Exhibition, October 1939, Second Honorable Mention, with Prize of $200, for *Bus Passengers.* Art Institute of Chicago, November 1940, Harris Bronze Medal and Prize of $300, for *Bus Passengers.* Pennsylvania Academy of the Fine Arts, January 1943, Temple Medal, for *Waiting Room.* Corcoran Gallery of Art, March 1943, Third W. A. Clark Prize of $1,000 and the Corcoran Bronze Medal, for *Waiting Room.* Artists for Victory, "America in the War," October 1943, Honorable Mention, for *Goodbye* (lithograph). Carnegie Institute, Painting in the United States, October 1944, Second Honorable Mention and $300 prize, for *Young Woman in Studio.* Pennsylvania Academy of the Fine Arts, January 1946, Lippincott Prize, $300, for *Patricia.* Corcoran Gallery of Art, April 1951, First W. A. Clark Prize, $2,000, and the Corcoran Gold Medal, for *Waiting for the Audition.* National Academy of Design, February 1957, Saltus Gold Medal for Merit, for *Still Life.* American Academy of Arts and Letters, May 1957, Award of Merit Medal for Painting and $1,000 Prize. Art:USA:59, April 1959, First Prize for Painting, $1,000, for *Pedestrians: Farewell to Lincoln Square.*

ILLUSTRATIONS

THE ARTIST'S PARENTS.
1932. Oil. 28 x 30.

UNDER THE BRIDGE.

c. 1932. Oil. 26¼ x 32⅛.
Collection of Dr. and Mrs. Arnold Lieber.

opposite: GITTEL.
1932. Oil. 49½ x 27¼.

31

INTIMATE INTERIOR.

c. 1933. Oil. $30\frac{1}{4}$ x $28\frac{1}{4}$.
Collection of Mr. and Mrs. Irving M. Ram.

Fé Alf and Her Pupils.

1935. Oil. 40 x 38.
The Newark Museum.

In the City Park.
c. 1934. Oil. 38 x 40.

READING FROM LEFT TO RIGHT.
c. 1936. Oil. 26¼ x 20¼.
Collection of Emil J. Arnold.

SHOP GIRLS.

c. 1936. Oil. 30 x 40.
Collection of Mr. and Mrs. Victor Beinfield.

TRANSIENTS.

1936. Oil. 37½ x 34⅛.
James A. Michener Foundation Collection, Allentown Art Museum.

Bus Passengers.

1938. Oil. 26 x 34.
Private collection.

Waiting Room.

c. 1940. Oil. 34¼ x 45¼.
The Corcoran Gallery of Art.

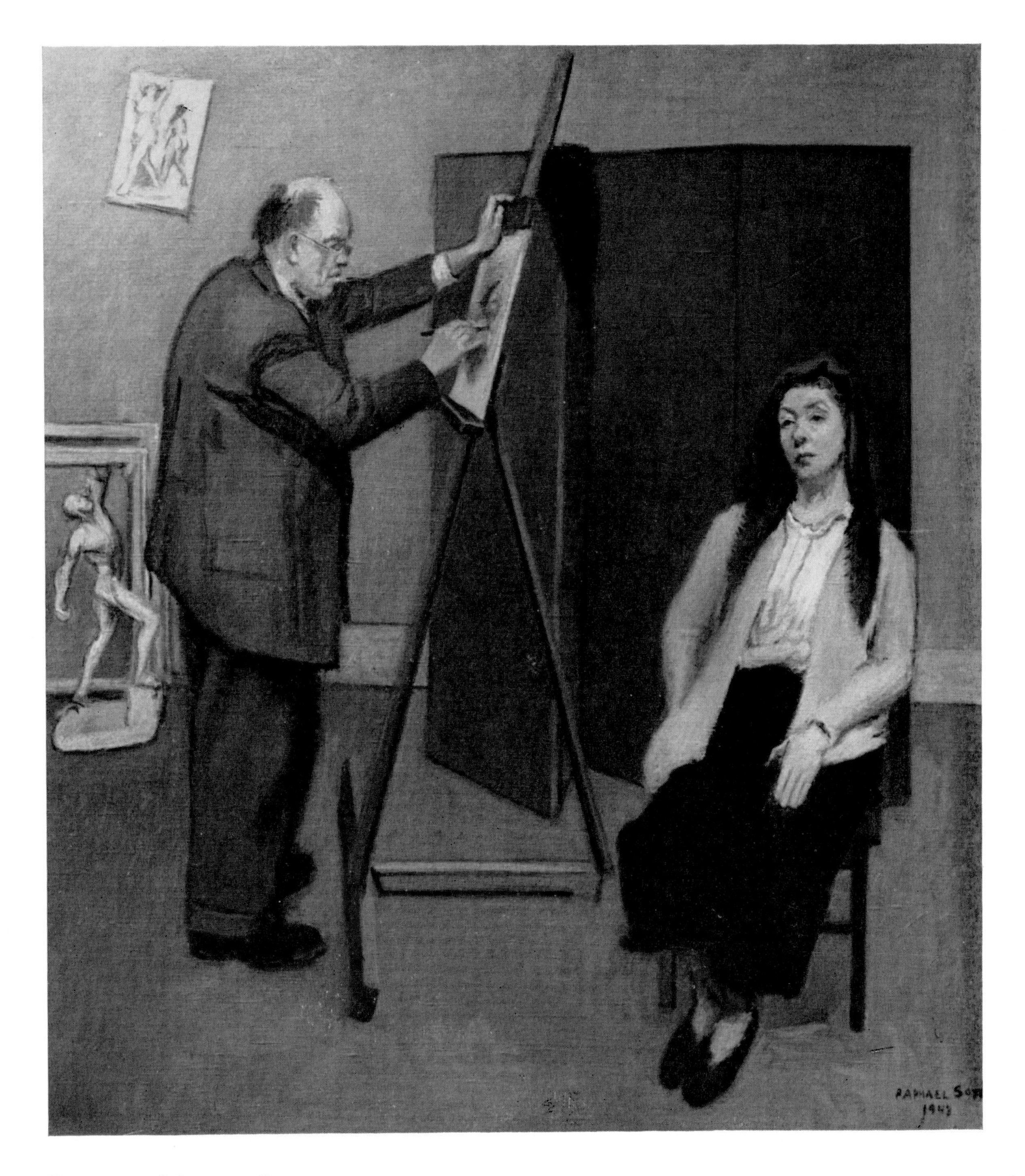

David and Marussia Burliuk.

1943. Oil. 26 x 22.
Joseph H. Hirshhorn Collection.

Young Woman in Studio.

1942. Oil. 39 x 29½.
Collection of Mrs. George G. Ornstein.

Office Girls.

1936. Oil. 26 x 24.
Whitney Museum of American Art.

In the Studio.

1943. Oil. 24 x 20.
Collection of Babette B. Newburger.

Maureen Stapleton.
c. 1946. Oil. 36 x 24.

JOSEPH STELLA.
c. 1940. Oil. 34 x 26.

THE SEAMSTRESS.

c. 1947. Oil. 25 x 30.
Collection of Mr. and Mrs. Warren Gold.

My Friends.

1948. Oil. 70 x 60.
The Butler Institute of American Art.

PENSIVE GIRL.

1946-47. Oil. 40 x 30.
Museum of Art, Carnegie Institute.

Dressmaker's Shop.
c. 1949. Oil. 39¼ x 35½.

CITY CHILDREN.

c. 1952. Oil. 47 x 37.
Collection of L. Arnold Weissberger.

opposite: THE BROWN SWEATER.

1952. Oil. 50 x 34.
Whitney Museum of American Ar

RAPHAEL
SOYER

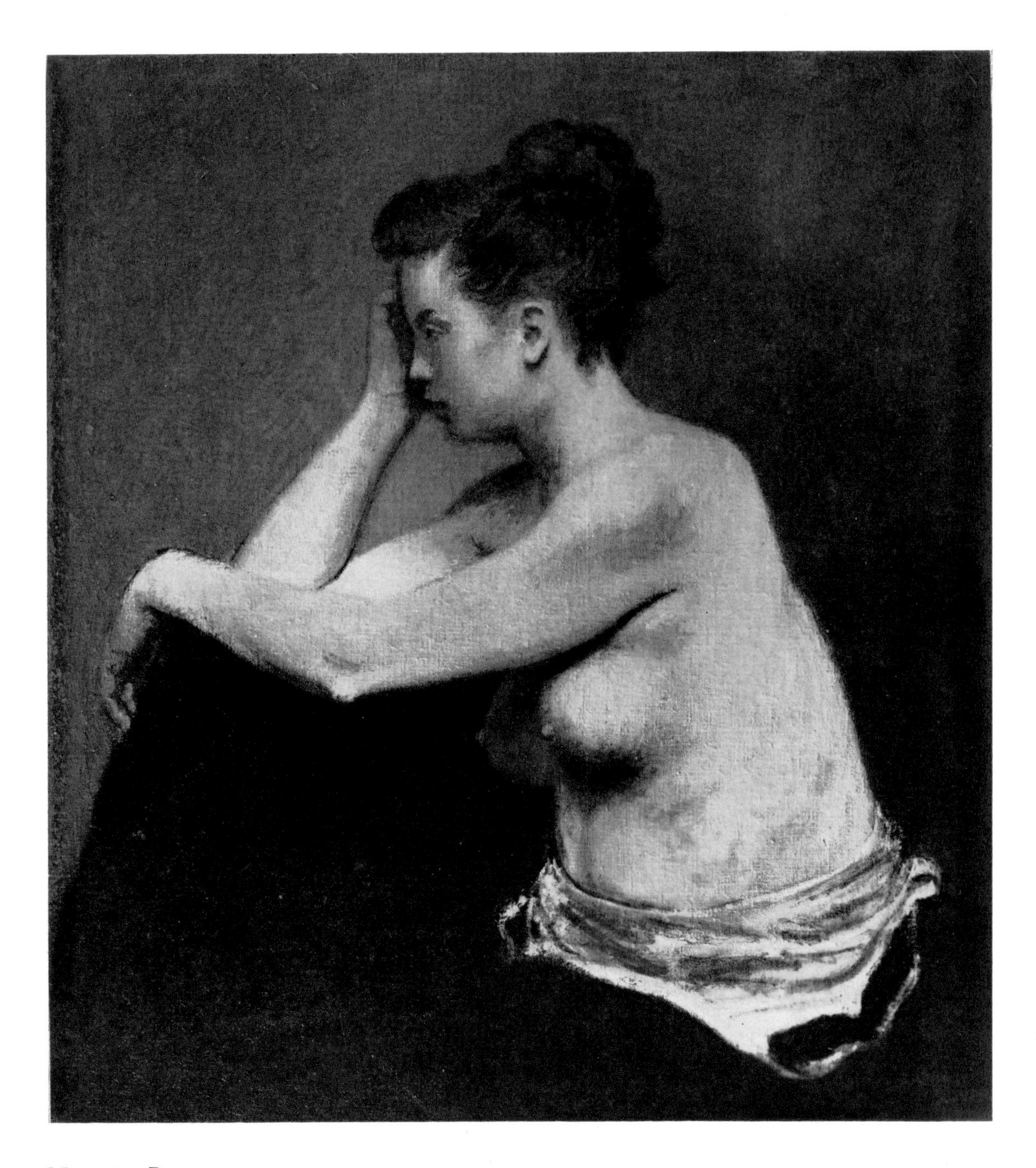

Nude in Profile.

1949. Oil. 40 x 34.
Collection of Mrs. Alma Walker.

Figures and Screen.
c. 1952. Oil. 40 x 30.

THE SCREEN.
1957. Oil. 40 x 36.

opposite: NUDE
c. 1952. Oil. 50 x 32.

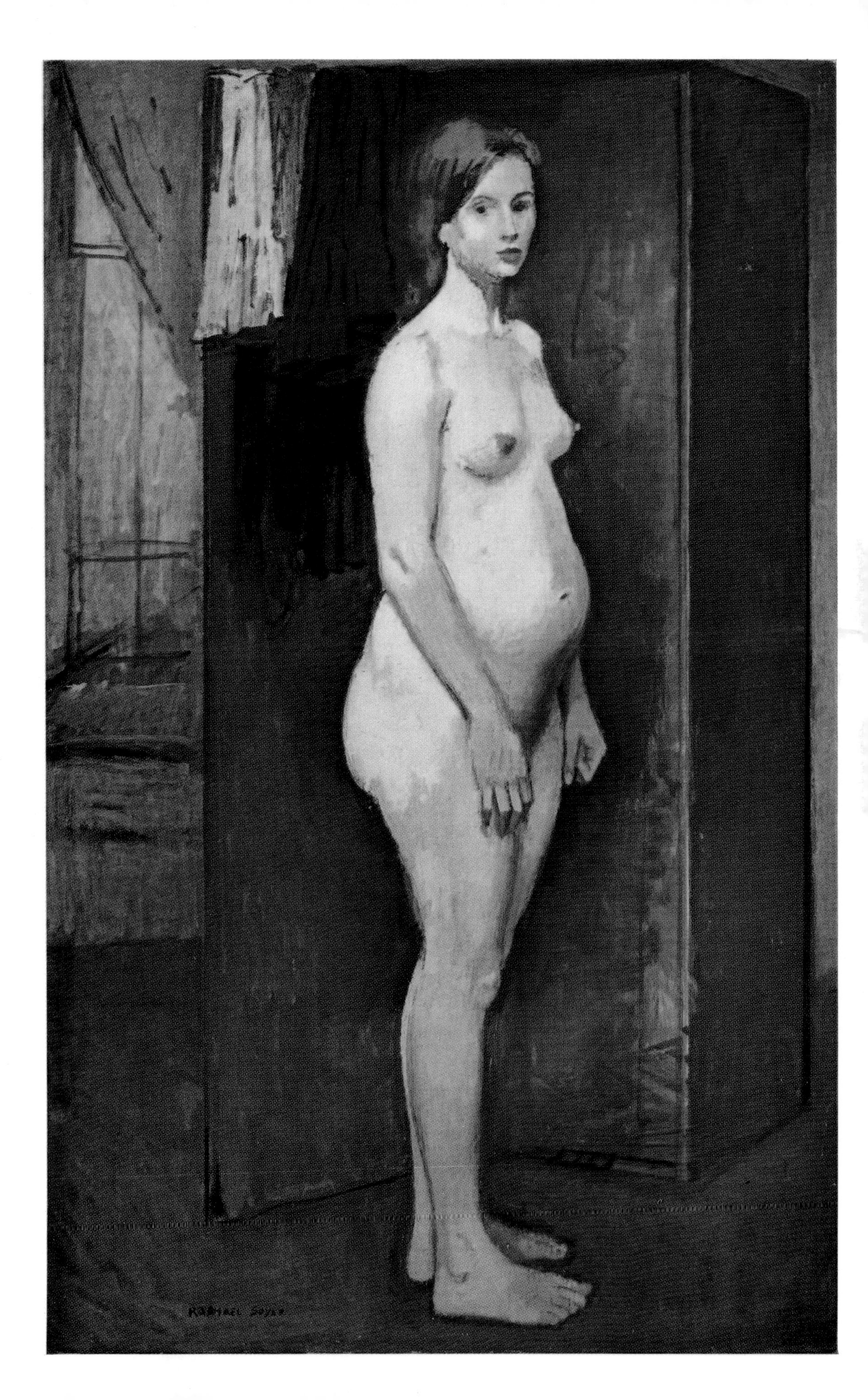

SEAMSTRESSES.

1953. Oil. 40 x 36.
Collection of Mr. and Mrs. Louis Friedenthal.

FIGURE.

c. 1955 Oil. 40 x 30.
Collection of Dr. Albert Ellis.

PEDESTRIANS.

c. 1959. Oil. 30 x 20.
Collection of Mr. and Mrs. Jack Wexler.

FAREWELL TO LINCOLN SQUARE.
1959. Oil. 60 x 55.
Joseph H. Hirshhorn Foundation.

Interior with Nude.

1958. Oil. 40 x 36.

Collection of Mr. and Mrs. M. A. Lipschultz.

61

SARAH JACKSON.
1964. Oil. 68 x 40.

MELANCHOLIA II.
1962. Oil. 38 x 34.

63

Standing Nude Female.

1960. Oil. 54½ x 32¼.
Krannert Art Museum, University of Illinois.

Life Studies for HOMAGE TO THOMAS EAKINS:
LLOYD GOODRICH. EDWARD HOPPER. LEONARD BASKIN. JACK LEVINE.
Joseph H. Hirshhorn Foundation.

HOMAGE TO THOMAS EAKINS.

1964-65. Oil. 88 x 80.

Joseph H. Hirshhorn Foundation.

Studies of Diane di Prima.
1965. Oil. 38 x 28.

Village East Street Scene.
1965-66. Oil. 60 x 60.
Collection of Joan and Lester Avnet.

DIANE DI PRIMA AND MINNIE.

1965. Oil. 35¼ x 23¼.
Collection of Mr. and Mrs. Dalton Trumbo.

Study for Village East Street Scene, II.
1965. Oil. 38 x 28.
Collection of Mr. and Mrs. Robert Goodman.

Cynthia.
1967. Oil. 46 x 50.

À Watteau.
1967. Oil. 50 x 40.

SELECTED BIBLIOGRAPHY

The place of publication is New York unless otherwise stated.

WRITINGS BY RAPHAEL SOYER

BOOKS

A Painter's Pilgrimage: an account of a journey with drawings by the author, 1962. 127 p., 46 il.

Homage to Thomas Eakins, Etc., by Raphael Soyer, edited by Rebecca L. Soyer, 1966. 183 p., 75 il.

PERIODICALS

Art Digest, v. 29, Nov. 15, 1953, p. 12, 33. "Symposium: The Human Figure."

Reality: A Journal of Artists' Opinions, No. 3, Summer 1955, p. 5-6. "Reginald Marsh: 1898-1954."

See also below: BOOKS: *Raphael Soyer,* 1946; *Raphael Soyer: Paintings and Drawings,* 1960; *Art USA Now,* 1962; EXHIBITION CATALOGUES: Associated American Artists Galleries, 1953; Montross Gallery, 1939; Newark Museum, 1944.

BOOKS

MONOGRAPHS ON RAPHAEL SOYER

Art Students League of New York: *Raphael Soyer: Instructor: Life Drawing: Painting: Composition,* n.d., c. 1933. 8 p., 8 il.

Raphael Soyer, American Artists Group, 1946. 64 p., 59 il. Text by Raphael Soyer, p. 3, 4, 6, 8.

Raphael Soyer: Paintings and Drawings, 1960. Text by Walter K. Gutman, Preface by Jerome Klein, Comments on Art by Raphael Soyer. 192 p., 166 il.

Raphael Soyer: Sixteen Etchings, Associated American Artists, 1965. Foreword by Carl Zigrosser (republished from *The Artist in America,* with additions). 24 p., 17 il.

Raphael Soyer: Fifty Years of Printmaking, 1917-1967, 1967. Foreword by Jacob Kainen.

BOOKS (GENERAL)

Art USA Now, v. 1, 1962. Edited by lee Nordness, text by Allen S. Weller. "Soyer" by Roland F. Pease, Jr., p. 86-89. Statement by Raphael Soyer, p. 87. 8 il.

Baur, John I. H.: *Revolution and Tradition in Modern American Art,* Cambridge, Mass., 1951, p. 19, 89, 90. 1 il.

Boswell, Peyton, Jr.: *Modern American Painting,* 1939, p. 190. 1 il.

Brown, Milton W.: *American Painting from the Armory Show to the Depression,* Princeton, N. J., 1955, p. 183, 184-185. 1 il.

Current Biography, edited by Maxine Block, 1941, p. 809-813. 3 il.

The Encyclopaedia Britannica Collection of Contemporary American Painting, written and edited by Grace Pagano, Chicago, 1946, pl. 113 and f. p.

Finkelstein, Sidney: *Realism in Art,* 1954, p. 169, 171.

Geldzahler, Henry: *American Painting in the Twentieth Century,* 1965, p. 109-110. 1 il.
Goodrich, Lloyd, and Baur, John I. H.: *American Art of Our Century,* 1961, p. 92, 126. 2 il.
Goodrich, Lloyd: *Three Centuries of American Art,* 1966, p. 77. 1 il.
Great Drawings of All Time, v. 4, selected and edited by Ira Moskowitz, 1962, pl. 1100.
Larkin, Oliver W.: *Art and Life in America,* 1949, 1960, p. 432-433. 1 il.
Mendelowitz, Daniel M.: *A History of American Art,* 1960, 1964, p. 575-576. 1 il.
Moses Soyer, 1962. Introduction by Charlotte Willard, Foreword by Philip Evergood.
Smith, Bernard: *Moses Soyer,* 1944.
Wheeler, Monroe: *20th Century Portraits,* 1942, p. 27. 3 il.
Zigrosser, Carl: *The Artist in America,* 1942, p. 55-61. 5 il.

EXHIBITION CATALOGUES

ONE-MAN EXHIBITIONS

Associated American Artists Galleries, 1953. Statement by Raphael Soyer. 5 il.
ACA Gallery, 1960. Text by Jerome Klein and Raphael Soyer (republished from Raphael Soyer: *Paintings and Drawings,* 1960). 5 il.
Forum Gallery, 1966. 9 il.

EXHIBITIONS (GENERAL)

Montross Gallery: *Exhibit of Paintings by Eight American Artists of Walter Broe,* 1939. Statement by Raphael Soyer. 1 il.
Carnegie Institute, Pittsburgh: *Survey of American Painting,* 1940. 1 il.
Newark Museum: *American Paintings and Sculpture,* 1944, p. 134-135. Introduction by Holger Cahill. Statement by Raphael Soyer. 1 il.
Brooklyn Museum: *The Herbert A. Goldstone Collection of American Art,* 1965, p. 91-93. 3 il.
American Federation of Arts: *American Masters: Art Students League,* 1967. "Raphael Soyer" by Lloyd Goodrich. 1 il.

PERIODICALS

AMERICAN ARTIST

v. 12, June 1948, p. 28-33, 64. Ernest W. Watson: "The Paintings of Raphael Soyer." 13 il.

AMERICAN MAGAZINE OF ART (later MAGAZINE OF ART)

v. 29, Dec. 1936, p. 818-819. F. A. Whiting, Jr.: "Two Versions of American Art." 1 il. (cover).
v. 32, April 1939, p. 201-207, 254, f. p. 195. Moses Soyer: "Three Brothers." 12 il.
v. 32, Nov. 1939, p. 629. Helen Buchalter: "Carnegie International, 1939." 1 il.

ART DIGEST (later ARTS DIGEST, ARTS, and ARTS MAGAZINE)

v. 7, March 1, 1933, p. 14. "New York Criticism."
v. 7, Sept. 1, 1933, p. 7. "Brook and Soyer Enter the Metropolitan." 1 il.
v. 8, Oct. 1, 1933, p. 25. "New Instructors at the Art Students League." 1 il.
v. 8, Feb. 15, 1934, p. 5-7. " 'Social Commentaries' Mark the Pennsylvania Academy's Annual." 1 il.
v. 9, March 1, 1935, p. 18. "New York Criticism."
v. 12, March 15, 1938, p. 12. "Raphael Soyer, Realist, Captures that 'Haunted Look of the Unemployed.' " 1 il.
v. 13, Nov. 1, 1938, p. 31. "The Scribner Covers." 1 il.
v. 15, April 1, 1941, p. 17. "Raphael Soyer Paints 23 Artists and Some Hungering Shop Girls." 3 il.
v. 18, March 15, 1944, p. 21. Maude Riley: "Fifty-Seventh Street in Review."
v. 22, March 1, 1948, p. 13. Margaret Breuning: "Raphael Soyer Shows Marked Advance." 1 il.
v. 25, April 15, 1951, p. 8, 28. Paul Bird: "A Soyer Profile." 1 il.
v. 27, April 15, 1953, p. 17. Margaret Breuning: "57th Street." 1 il.
v. 31, Dec. 1956, p. 50. "Margaret Breuning Writes." 1 il.
v. 32, Nov. 1957, p. 50. "Margaret Breuning Writes."

v. 35, Jan. 1961, p. 47. Sidney Tillim: "Month in Review." 1 il.

ART IN AMERICA

v. 53, No. 3, June 1965, p. 92. Cleve Gray: "The Portfolio Collector." 1 il.

ART NEWS

v. 30, Feb. 27, 1932, p. 10. "Around the Galleries."

v. 31, Feb. 18, 1933, p. 5. "Exhibitions in New York."

v. 32, Jan. 6, 1934, cover.

v. 32, Jan. 13, 1934, p. 13. Richard Beer: "As They Are at Thirty-Four." 1 il.

v. 33, Feb. 23, 1935, p. 10. Laurie Eglington: "Exhibitions in New York."

v. 33, March 30, 1935, p. 13. Laurie Eglington: "Exhibitions in New York."

v. 36, March 12, 1938, p. 13. James Lane: "New Exhibitions of the Week."

v. 37, April 15, 1939, p. 14. "New Exhibitions of the Week."

v. 40, April 1-14, 1941, p. 29. James Lane: "The Passing Shows." 1 il.

v. 43, March 15-31, 1944, p. 20. "The Passing Shows."

v. 47, April 1948, p. 51. "Reviews and Previews."

v. 52, May 1953, p. 44. Fairfield Porter: "Reviews and Previews."

v. 55, Dec. 1956, p. 13. Herbert D. Hale: "Reviews and Previews." 1 il.

v. 59, Dec. 1960, p. 35, 52. Lawrence Campbell: "Raphael Soyer's own brand of realism." 1 il.

v. 65, May 1966, p. 22. John Perreault: "Reviews and Previews." 1 il.

THE ARTS

v. 15, May 1929, p. 334. Lloyd Goodrich: "Exhibitions in New York." 1 il.

BURLINGTON MAGAZINE, London

Jan. 1961. Stuart Preston: "Current and Forthcoming Exhibitions."

CREATIVE ART

v. 6, April 1930, p. 258-260. Walter Gutman: "Raphael Soyer." 2 il.

v. 10, March 1932, p. 233. C. Adolph Glassgold: "Around the Galleries." 1 il.

v. 12, March 1933, p. 240, 243. Edwina Spencer: "Around the Galleries." Walter Gutman: "News and Gossip." 1 il.

ESQUIRE

v. 9, May 1938, p. 58-61, 155-158. Harry Salpeter: "Raphael Soyer: East Side Degas." 14 il.

FORTUNE

v. 12, Dec. 1935, p. 68, 71. "U. S. Art, 1935; In the City Park: Raphael Soyer." 1 il.

THE NEW YORKER

March 19, 1938, p. 54-55. Robert M. Coates: "The Art Galleries."

March 18, 1944, p. 76. Robert M. Coates: "The Art Galleries."

March 13, 1948, p. 61-62. Robert M. Coates: "Latter-Day Impressionist."

NEWSWEEK

v. 41, April 6, 1953, p. 54. "Painter of Solitude."

PARNASSUS

v. 7, March 1935, p. 25, 31. "Current Exhibitions."

v. 10, March 1938, p. 20. Margaret Breuning: "Art in New York." 1 il.

v. 13, April 1941, p. 158. Milton Brown: "Exhibitions–New York."

SCRIBNER'S MAGAZINE

v. 100, Nov. 1936, p. 30-31. "Scribner's Presents Raphael Soyer." 3 il.

v. 104, Nov. 1938, cover, p. 4. "Portrait of an Agitator." 1 il.

SURVEY GRAPHIC

v. 29, Jan. 1940, p. 17. "In the ig City: Paintings by Raphael Soyer." 2 il.

TIME

v. 51, March 22, 1948, p. 59-60. "Unhappy Angels." 1 il.

v. 76, Dec. 12, 1960, p. 78. "Oblivious People." 1 il.

v. 85, March 26, 1965, p. 70-73. "Unlikely Likenesses." 1 il.

ACKNOWLEDGMENTS

This monograph is published on the occasion of the first full-scale retrospective exhibition of Raphael Soyer's work, organized by the Whitney Museum of American Art in the fall of 1967, and shown subsequently in six other museums throughout the United States.

The author wishes to express his great indebtedness to Raphael Soyer and to Mrs. Soyer for their cooperation in making his paintings and drawings available for study, and in supplying information about the present ownership of works in private hands. I particularly appreciate the artist's kindness in allowing me to read the manuscript of his forthcoming book, which furnished much first-hand autobiographical material. The Whitney Museum also wishes to thank Mr. and Mrs. Soyer for their generosity in lending works to the retrospective exhibition.

To Mrs. Bella Fishko, Director of the Forum Gallery, we want to express our warm gratitude for her constant help throughout the planning of the exhibition. We are especially grateful to her for bringing together for study many works from private collections.

Special thanks are due to Abram Lerner, Curator of the Joseph H. Hirshhorn Foundation; to Emil J. Arnold, Alfredo Valente and Julius Zirinsky; to Geoffrey Clements who did all the color photography; and to Miss Estelle Yanco of Associated American Artists, Inc., for information about the artist's prints.

In all aspects of the exhibition and monograph I have had the invaluable help of Mrs. Patricia FitzGerald Mandel, Research Curator of the Whitney Museum, who selected the watercolors, drawings and prints; and of her Assistant, Mrs. Annabelle S. Bullen, who helped greatly with research.

On behalf of the Whitney Museum I wish to thank the following museums and collectors whose generosity in lending works made the retrospective exhibition possible:

Allentown Art Museum, the James A. Michener Foundation Collection; The Butler Institute of American Art, Youngstown, Ohio; Museum of Art, Carnegie Institute, Pittsburgh; The Corcoran Gallery of Art, Washington, D. C.; The Detroit Institute of Arts; Fogg Art Museum, Harvard University; Krannert Art Museum, University of Illinois, Champaign; The Metropolitan Museum of Art, New York; University Gallery, University of Minnesota, Duluth; The Montclair Art Museum, N. J.; The Museum of Modern Art, New York; Nebraska Art Association, University of Nebraska, Lincoln; The New York Public Library; The Newark Museum; The Phillips Collection, Washington, D. C.

Emil J. Arnold; Joan and Lester Avnet Collection; Mr. and Mrs. Victor Beinfield; Mrs. George Boynton; Gladys and Selig Burrows; Margit Winter Chanin, Ltd.; Mr. and Mrs. David G. Cohen; Mr. and Mrs. Aaron W. Davis; Mr. and Mrs. Albert J. Dreitzer; Dr. Albert Ellis; Dr. and Mrs. S. N. Feinsod; Mr. and Mrs. Jay Folb; Mr. and Mrs. S. Foster; Mr. and Mrs. Louis Friedenthal; Mr. and Mrs. Warren Gold; Mr. and Mrs. Herbert A. Goldstone; Mr. and Mrs. Robert Goodman; Renée and Chaim Gross; S. J. Gross; Mr. and Mrs. Samuel Halpern; Mrs. Nathan E. Handler; Joseph H. Hirshhorn Collection; Joseph H. Hirshhorn Foundation; Mr. and Mrs. Oliver Lazare; Dr. and

Mrs. Arnold Lieber; Mr. and Mrs. M. A. Lipschultz Collection; Earle Ludgin; Mr. and Mrs. Roy R. Neuberger; Babette B. Newburger; Mrs. George G. Ornstein; Bernard A. Osher; Mr. and Mrs. Irving M. Ram; Mr. and Mrs. Tony Randall; Mr. and Mrs. Neil Reisner; Mr. and Mrs. Charles H. Renthal; Mr. and Mrs. Herbert M. Sandler; Mr. and Mrs. Emil Schlesinger; Mr. and Mrs. Herb Schneyer; Mr. and Mrs. Milton Schwartz; Mr. and Mrs. Samuel Shore; Mr. and Mrs. Herbert M. Singer; David and Janet Soyer; Mr. and Mrs. Dalton Trumbo; Mr. and Mrs. Alfredo Valente; Dr. and Mrs. J. J. Vargish; Dr. and Mrs. Seymour Wadler; Mrs. Alma Walker; L. Arnold Weissberger; Mr. and Mrs. Jack Wexler; Mr. and Mrs. Julius Zirinsky.

INDEX OF ILLUSTRATIONS

OILS

WATERCOLORS

DRAWINGS

PRINTS